basketball's new wave

Tim Duncan

Tower of Power

BY
MARK STEWART

THE MILLBROOK PRESS
BROOKFIELD, CONNECTICUT

THE MILLBROOK PRESS

Produced by
BITTERSWEET PUBLISHING
John Sammis, President
and
TEAM STEWART, INC.

Series Design and Electronic Page Makeup by
JAFFE ENTERPRISES
Ron Jaffe

Researched and Edited by
Mariah Morgan

All photos courtesy
AP/ Wide World Photos, Inc.
except the following:
Rich Kane/SportsChrome — Cover
The following image is from the collection of Team Stewart:
Sports Illustrated, Time Inc. (1986) — inset page 36

Printed in the United States of America

Published by
The Millbrook Press, Inc.
2 Old New Milford Road
Brookfield, Connecticut 06804

Visit us at our web site – http://www.millbrookpress.com

Library of Congress Cataloging-in-Publication Data

Stewart, Mark.
   Tim Duncan:tower of power / by Mark Stewart [researched and edited by Mariah Morgan]
   p.   cm.   — (Basketball's new wave)
   Includes index.
   Summary: Presents a biography of the San Antonio Spurs center, who chose to stay in school and get his college degree before joining the NBA.
   ISBN 0-7613-1513-6 (lib. bdg.)   ISBN 0-7613-1041-X (pbk.)
   1. Duncan, Tim, 1976 –   —Juvenile literature. Basketball players—United States—Biography—
Juvenile literature. [1. Duncan, Tim, 1976 –   . 2. Basketball players. 3. Blacks—Virgin Islands of the
United States—Biography.] I. Morgan, Mariah. II. Series.
GV884.D86D84 1999
796.323'092--dc21
[B]
                                                                    98-32237
                                                                        CIP
                                                                         AC

Contents

chapter 1

Different Strokes

"He would have gone to the 1992 Olympics and held his own against the world."
— TRICIA DUNCAN

Confidence and vision have never been in short supply in the Duncan family. Nor has athletic ability. What few NBA fans know, however, is that Tim Duncan was headed for international superstardom in a sport other than basketball. You see, until a strange and tragic series of events touched Tim and his family, his path to greatness could not have been clearer. He was one of the best young swimmers on earth.

"Timmy was even better than me," claims Tricia, his sister. That's saying something, for she was a champion swimmer herself. In 1988, Tricia went to Seoul, South Korea, to compete in the Olympics. Then she passed the torch to her little brother, who was lighting it up in his specialty, the 400-meter freestyle. How good was he? It takes a little prodding to find out.

"People knew who I was," admits Tim. "I was pretty good for my age."

Tim has become one of the top players in basketball.
A decade ago, however, his future appeared to be in swimming.

"Tim has always underestimated himself," his father, William, says, pointing out that he held several records as a 13- and 14-year-old. "He was world-class. He had talked about the Olympics since he was 10 years old. I think he would have won the gold medal."

The truth? It probably lies somewhere between "pretty good" and "world-class." And that is essentially where Tim Duncan's story begins.

He was born and raised on St. Croix, an 82-square-mile (212-square-km) Caribbean paradise just east of Puerto Rico. St. Croix is part of the U.S. Virgin Islands. The Crucians (as they call themselves) speak English, use dollars, and watch American television shows. Life on St. Croix is dominated by water. Not surprisingly, some of the best athletes on the island are swimmers.

All three Duncan kids were. Cheryl, the eldest, blazed the trail. Tricia, who specialized in the 100- and 200-meter backstroke, ranked among the best in the world. And Tim's times put him on par with the top young swimmers in the United States.

Tim powered his long, supple body through the water with strong, measured strokes and fierce concentration. Behind his every kick was his mother, Ione, who attended all of his meets and gave him little tidbits of advice and inspiration with a nervous, machine-gun delivery that sometimes drove her son crazy. "She was my biggest fan," Tim remembers. "Every meet she was the loudest parent there. Somehow I could always pick out her voice yelling over everybody else."

Ione, a professional midwife, was coach, manager, traveling secretary, and treasurer of "Team Duncan," and she adored every minute of it. Ione was also the team psychiatrist. She made certain that her children understood that her love was unconditional, and that her respect was not a function of how many trophies they won, but of how hard they tried. Her motto was: *Good, better, best. Never let it rest. Until your good is better, and your better is best.*

"He's a great player, there's not any question about that."
NBA COACH JERRY SLOAN

Tim gets his competitive fire from his mother, Ione.

Wipe Out

chapter 1

"It's just something that was a part of me and went away."

— TIM DUNCAN

As years go, 1989 was stacking up very nicely for the Duncans. Tim's dad, William, a mason, was busy at work, Ione was delivering a lot of healthy babies, Tricia was getting on with her career, and Cheryl was happily married and living in Columbus, Ohio. As for Tim, he was shaving seconds off his times in the 50, 100, and 400 meters. He was a lock to make the Virgin Islands Olympic team in 1992, and possibly the U.S. team.

Tim, however, was more concerned with enjoying life as a laid-back 13-year-old on a laid-back island. He hung out with his friends, listened to Reggae music, and once in a while would pick up a basketball and toss it at the rim and backboard that Cheryl had sent the previous Christmas. Tim's father had gone to great pains to set it up precisely at the regulation height of 10 feet (3 m). When he finished, William looked at it proudly and told Tim it would stand up to any hurricane that hit the island.

Unfortunately, the storm clouds were starting to gather. That summer, Ione discovered a strange lump in her body. She was diagnosed with breast cancer and started to undergo treatment at the hospital in St. Dunstan's.

On the evening of September 17, hurricane Hugo laid a direct hit on St. Croix. The Duncans huddled together in their house, wondering whether they would live or die. They could hear the bedlam outside—branches cracking, neighbors screaming, and loud thuds as objects big and small slammed into the side of their home. "It was very scary," Tim says. "You could hear the trees snapping. I had never experienced anything like that."

Tim looked at his father, trying to detect any signs of fear. He could see none. "He had been through a couple of them," Tim smiles. "Seeing him, I felt all right."

When Hugo passed, the Duncans ventured outside to survey the damage. Their home had come through the hurricane with only minor damage. The house next door, however, had no roof. Debris was strewn all over the town. Boats from the harbor were piled up in the streets like toys. Tim went to the pool where he trained. It was destroyed. The swim team's coach decided to move training to the ocean, but Tim—who had a mortal fear of sharks—was not crazy about this idea. He began skipping practices and slowly drifted from the sport.

On April 24, 1990—a day before Tim turned 14—Ione Duncan died. She had continued to work until the end, bringing as much life into the world as she could before she drew her last breath. Tim's biggest fan was gone. He never swam competitively again.

> ## Did You Know?
>
> When Tim was eight, he skipped from the second grade to the fourth. He was a year younger than his classmates right through college.

"I've never gotten too high or too low. It only messes you up."
TIM DUNCAN (WITH SAN ANTONIO SPURS COACH GREGG POPOVICH)

Tim developed his power game in college. As a kid, he focused
more on his play around the perimeter.

Dunkin' Duncan

chapter

"Some things come easy to me."

— **TIM DUNCAN**

he silver lining in the dark cloud of Ione's death was that Cheryl and her husband, Ricky Lowery, moved back from Ohio to stay with Tim and his dad. While attending Capital University in Columbus, Ricky was the starting point guard for the Crusaders. Fearing his nephew would soon lose all interest in sports, he began bugging Tim to shoot some hoops. Eventually, he gave in. Although Tim had fooled around with basketball in the past, until his one-on-ones with Ricky, he never gave the game much thought.

Tim was tall for his age—around 6 feet (183 cm)—but there was nothing to suggest that he would one day be 7 feet (213 cm) tall. Ricky guessed that Tim might top out at 6 feet 5 or 6 feet 6 (196 or 198 cm), so he decided to teach Tim the perimeter game: ball-handling, passing, penetrating, coming off screens, three-point shooting, and medium-range jumpers. That fall, Tim made the St. Dunstan's Episcopal High School team as a 14-year-old freshman. "I remember thinking that after the basketball season ended I'd go back to swimming," he says. "But then basketball season never ended!"

chapter 4 Discovered

"He was almost colt-like. Very young, but with unique, natural skills that would develop quickly."

— **DAVE ODOM, WAKE FOREST UNIVERSITY COACH**

By the end of his junior year, Tim was the best player on the island. He also had grown 9 more inches (23 cm). Tim's outside game was superb from his training as a guard, and now his inside game was beginning to take off. He did not always understand what he was doing, but he used his body and moved his feet in just the right way to establish position inside. Tim was a "raw" talent who had no access to top-level competition or coaching, yet in many ways he was far more advanced than his counterparts in the United States. In retrospect, he had enjoyed a rare luxury: He had learned basketball in his own way, at his own pace.

Three U.S. schools got wind of Tim during his junior season. The University of Hartford, the University of Delaware, and Providence University had heard the kind of crazy stories coaches often receive from basketball backwaters like St. Croix. Something about a 6 foot 10 (208 cm) Olympic swimmer with an uncle who used to play guard for a Division-III school. Still, any big man was worth a look, so each college sent someone down to scout Tim.

Then a fourth school entered the picture. Dave Odom, coach of Wake Forest University in Winston-Salem, North Carolina, contacted the Duncans and made arrangements to come down, meet Tim, and watch him play. Odom was on a quest to recruit big men for his Demon Deacons. The team had a wonderful guard named

Wake Forest coach Dave Odom

Randolph Childress, but lacked a dominant presence inside. Odom was not afraid to go outside the mainland United States (he had already two players from Africa and Europe), so St. Croix was a relatively short trip. Still, when he arrived on the island, he was wondering whether the trip was worthwhile.

All Odom had to go on before seeing Tim face-to-face was a rave review he had received from a former Wake Forest player named Chris King. Earlier in the year, King had been touring with a group of young NBA players, and during a stopover in St. Croix they slapped together a game with some of the local talent. Tim, just a few months past his 16th birthday, was given the unenviable task of guarding Alonzo Mourning. Mourning had just been selected by the Charlotte Hornets with the second pick in the 1992 NBA Draft. Tim battled the All-American at both ends, giving as good as he got, and making some big-time plays. King got on the phone to Odom immediately, and the wheels started turning.

Odom was relieved to see Tim at the airport. At least he was around 6-10, as he had been promised. But the coach became anxious when he learned that the game he had come all this way to watch would be played outdoors, and was little more than a glorified pick-up affair. He knew that if a cloudburst came, the players would scatter and his trip would be a waste. Tim sensed Odom's dismay, and before the game began he leaned over and said, "No matter what happens out there, I just want you to know I can play this game." Then he proceeded to put on a show.

That evening, in the Duncan home, Odom made his pitch. He talked about the Wake Forest campus, the learning environment, the team, the region—anything he could think of to sway Tim. The only problem was that the young man did not appear to be listening. Instead, his eyes kept drifting over to the television. "The 49ers game was on," Tim laughs. "And it was the fourth quarter."

Odom, desperate to get Tim's attention, kept moving closer to the screen. Finally, he asked if he could turn off the TV. He told Tim he was afraid he wasn't listening. "He repeated back to me word-for-word what I had been telling him," smiles Odom. "I was amazed. He had this innate ability to look distracted, but still take in everything around him."

Tim liked what he heard from Coach Odom, and thanked him for coming. He wanted to take his time with the decision, he said. A month later, he made up his mind: He would attend Wake Forest in the fall. Free to enjoy his senior year, Tim averaged 25 points, 12 rebounds, and 5 block per game.

Tim introduces his father, William, to the Wake Forest crowd.

Fresh
Frosh

chapter 6

"He doesn't know how good he is yet."

— DICK VITALE

im's first college game came against the University of Alaska in Anchorage. It was the first time time he had ever seen snow, and the first time he was held scoreless on a basketball court. For the first half of Tim's freshman year, in fact, Tim rarely asserted himself. He was more of a spectator than a contributor, working hard in practice, playing hard against Wake's opponents, but never really taking control. Slowly and quietly, however, Tim was learning.

Wake Forest's record stood at an impressive 10-2 when it began conference play. Big wins over ACC rivals Florida State, Duke, and Georgia Tech—and a near miss against Maryland—had everyone excited. So did Tim, who was beginning to show flashes of brilliance.

At other times, however, he seemed overwhelmed. In a game at Clemson, Coach Odom watched with concern as his young center was schooled by Sharone Wright. "It was a man against a young boy," recalls Odom, "one thunder dunk after another."

ESPN commentator Dick Vitale knows a star in the making when he sees one. He raved about Tim after watching him his freshman year.

Tim spent much of his freshman year watching and learning.
By season's end he was a dominant inside player.
Tim wore # 21 as a freshman, and has worn that number ever since.

After the team returned to campus, Tim got a message to report to the coach's office. After a few moments, he realized Odom wasn't going to chew him out. He was concerned that Tim was shell-shocked. Tim smiled and assured him that he was fine. He was learning and having a great time!

Tim turned it on and was sensational the rest of the way. The Deacons scored major wins over Top 10 teams Duke and North Carolina, and earned a bid to the NCAA Tournament on the strength of their impressive 20-11 record. And for the first time, Tim was being mentioned along

with the top freshmen in the country. His comfort level on the perimeter was what first caught people's attention, but what excited coaches and scouts most was that he exhibited pivot moves that normally take years to teach. The footwork, positioning—the subtle use of the hips and lower body—were already there.

Wake's NCAA Tournament run lasted just two games, as the Deacons were eliminated by Kansas. But Tim's season was an unqualified success. In 33 games he had swatted 124 shots, and he dominated on the defensive boards. He averaged just under 10 points and 10 rebounds a game and hit well over half his shots from the floor.

Tim came on so strong at the end of his freshman season that he received a last-minute invitation to play for Team USA at the Goodwill Games. Imagine going from "mystery man" to center on the national team in the span of a few short months. It was quite a year.

""He's a quiet assassin who is skilled in all aspects of the game."
NBA COACH GEORGE KARL

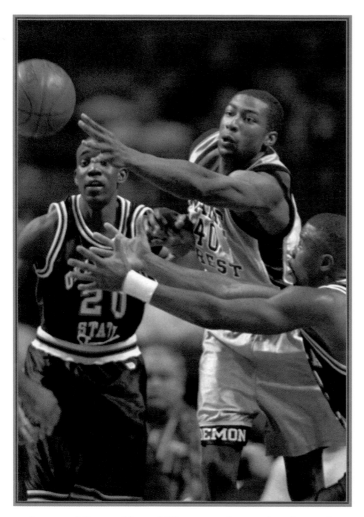

Forward Sean Allen (40) was a key role player in Wake Forest's 1994–95 ACC championship.

down 20 rebounds. It wasn't until Childress canned a short jumper with four seconds left in overtime, however, that the game was decided. In two short seasons, Wake Forest had gone from worst to first in the ACC.

In the NCAA Tournament, the Deacons did well until they met Oklahoma State. It was a furious defensive battle between two similar teams, and the game seesawed back and forth until an uncharacteristic turnover by Childress decided it. Tim grabbed 22 rebounds, rejected eight shots, and limited Bryant "Big Country" Reeves to just four baskets in 15 attempts. But it wasn't enough, and the Deacons lost 71-66.

That game proved to Tim that staying in college was the right move. Although the numbers say he manhandled Reeves, he knew just the opposite was true. Reeves, an NBA-bound senior, had pushed Tim around all game. He tried to imagine a league with 20 or 30 guys bigger than Big Country, and what it would be like to have to play them night after night after night. "I was not ready," Tim says. "I just felt I was too young to be in the NBA."

Tim's sophomore numbers were exceptional. He averaged 16.8 points and 12.5 rebounds a game, doubled his assist total from the year before, and shot 59 percent from the floor. He was named the top defensive player in the country and earned All-

ACC honors. And after two seasons, he owned the third-highest blocks-per-game average (3.98) in NCAA history.

That June, Joe Smith was the first selection in the NBA draft, chosen by the Golden State Warriors. Dave Twardzik, the team's general manager, would have opted for Tim had he been available, saying a month before the draft, "He's the best in college—it's not even close."

Joe Smith entered the NBA draft after his sophomore year.

"I have seen the future and he wears number 21."
NBA SUPERSTAR CHARLES BARKLEY

Tim and guard Tony Rutland helped Wake win its second ACC title in 1996.

Stayin' in School

chapter 8

> "Mom never got to see Timmy play ball seriously. But I think she's looking down from heaven cheering him on—the loudest voice among all the angels."
>
> — *CHERYL DUNCAN LOWERY*

Tim was a man on a mission in 1995–96. Having had a taste of the ACC championship, he was hungry for more. With Childress graduated and in a Portland Trail Blazers uniform, the team's backcourt would consist of sophomores Jerry Braswell and Tony Rutland. Rutland, the point guard, had only played the position for one full season, and that was in high school. He had been forced into the role when teammate Allen Iverson was suspended for a year for his part in an infamous bowling alley brawl. Braswell, a former point guard, had only recently switched to shooting guard. Wake's inexperience on the perimeter would mean Tim could expect to see a lot of double- and triple-teams. The biggest challenge for Tim, however, would be to step into the leadership role vacated by Childress.

Tim's first gesture as Wake Forest's new floor leader was to sacrifice some numbers early in the season so that his teammates—particularly the sophomore guards—could get more involved and gain more confidence. Thanks to Tim's unselfishness, by the time the ACC schedule got under way, the Deacons were a cohesive and self-assured unit. That season, Tim left no doubt as to who was the top player in the conference.

Did You Know?

Tim has a sharp eye when it comes to collecting. He owns several valuable old knives, as well as an authentic Japanese samurai sword.

His court vision—already considered the best among college pivotmen—showed great improvement over the year before. Tim also worked some kinks out of his turnaround jumper, and developed a reliable left-handed jump-hook. In the ACC Tournament, the Deacons beat Virginia and Clemson, then won a nail-biter against Georgia Tech to win the title for the second year in a row. In that game, Tim scored 27 points and had 22 rebounds.

Wake entered the NCAA Tournament with some problems. Tim was battling the flu, and Rutland was hobbled by a knee injury. Still, after beating Northeast Louisiana, Texas, and Louisville, the Deacons were looking like a decent bet to go all the way. Unfortunately, the team ran into Rick Pitino's Kentucky Wildcats. The Wildcats did not really have a first-rate big man to deal with Tim, so they triple-teamed him most of the game.

All season long, Tim's teammates had come through in this type of situation, taking his quick passes and hitting open shots. On this night, however, the strategy failed. Pitino dared the Deacons to win the game, and they blew it, missing dozens of easy jumpers. Kentucky's approach was so effective that Tim managed only seven shots the whole game. "That was the best defense I ever saw," he says. "Everybody was moving all the time, everybody was so athletic. They didn't give me anything."

The moment Wake's season ended, everyone's attention turned to whether Tim would go pro. Coach Odom asked to be the first to know when Tim made up his mind, and Tim agreed. On May 8, Odom called Tim from his car phone. Tim was sitting at the coach's desk. Coach Odom had set it up this way because he could not bear the suspense and did not want to be in the same room when Tim decided. Tim had two sheets of paper in front of him. One was a press release announcing that he had left Wake Forest to go pro. The other announced that he had decided to stay. Tim read them both, waited just long enough to give Odom heart failure, then told him he would stay.

The rest of the team was ecstatic about the news. "It was a great relief," remembers forward Sean Allen. "Like hearing that somebody you love had made it through surgery. It's like the whole team was pacing nervously in the waiting room. But I think Coach Odom was working the worry beads the hardest!"

What made Tim stay? He claims *The Hurried Child* by David Elkind convinced him that, at 20, he was still too young for the NBA. The book discusses the perils of forcing big responsibilities on young people before they are ready, and this made a great impression on Tim.

Coach Odom feels it goes deeper than that. "His father and mother were both

Tim recovered from the flu to slam-dunk Louisville in the 1996 NCAA Tournament.

very committed to education," he recalls. "But I think even more than that, they were committed to being yourself, taking your time and not rushing nature—I think that was in him before he got to Wake Forest."

In 1996–97, Tim averaged
20 points a game for the first time
in his college career.

job fell to Peral, who stayed in motion all night long and ran the Utes' superstar ragged. Utah, in return, attempted to smother Tim, as Kentucky had in the NCAAs. That's when Tim unveiled a new move, putting the ball on the floor and slicing through three defenders. When a fourth man cut between him and the basket, Tim shoveled a soft pass to Woods for an easy bucket. The NBA scouts scribbled madly in their notebooks. What Tim had just done is something it takes years to teach an NBA center, and most never learn. Tim's "swish-and-dish" show went on all game long, as he finished with 8 assists, 23 points and 18 rebounds in an impressive win for the Deacons.

Tim would have had a few more assists in the game, but his teammates were not hitting a high percentage of their open shots. Coach Odom worried about this, and with

Did You Know?

Tim may hold the record for toughest courses taken while winning NCAA Player of the Year. As a senior at Wake Forest, he took anthropology, psychology, and Chinese literature.

good reason. As the season wore on, the shooters wore down, particularly in the final minutes of close games. By the time the ACC Tournament neared, Tim's teammates were struggling to hit more than a third of their shots, and they were making a lot of bad turnovers.

Although Tim continued to play magnificently, his supporting cast did not. Wake Forest failed to win its third consecutive ACC championship, falling to North Carolina. In the NCAA Tournament, the Deacons met an underrated Stanford squad in the second round. The Cardinal, led by guard Brevin Knight, did exactly what Wake was supposed to: eliminate turnovers and make jumpshots. Tim watched helplessly as Stanford did everything right and Wake did everything wrong. Wake's 72-66 loss marked the final game of Tim Duncan's college career.

The Duncan File

TIM'S FAVORITE...

Meal: . . . . .Tex-Mex or Steak
Dessert: . . . . .Rainbow Sherbet
Hobby: . . . . .Video Games
Music: . . . . Reggae
Movie: . . . . *The Crow*
Animated Character: . . . . . The Tick
Shirt: . . . . .Sleeveless T
School Subject: . . . . . .Psychology*

* Earned a bachelor's degree from Wake Forest

In his rookie season, Tim participated in the various community programs organized by the Spurs in and around San Antonio. Going forward, he hopes to assume a leadership role in the fight against cancer, and plans to work with kids who have lost a parent to the disease.

Special Issue COLLEGE BASKETBALL 1986-87
North Carolina Is No.1   Bob Knight's Season On The Brink

Sports Illustrated

TOP GUN

NAVY'S
DAVID
ROBINSON

The Admiral

chapter 11

"I've tried to help Tim understand that if you don't prepare yourself, you won't perform well. Most of what you do on the floor comes from preparation."

— **DAVID ROBINSON**

im had good reason to be happy about joining the Spurs. The top picks in previous seasons (Allen Iverson, Joe Smith, Glenn Robinson) had gone to rebuilding or disintegrating teams, and the pressure on these young stars had been unbearable at times. San Antonio was a different story. Their poor record from the previous season was a result of the team's 32-year-old center, David Robinson, missing all but six games due to a back injury. The Spurs' 20 wins may have represented a franchise low, but it came with a bright side: Tim Duncan.

David Robinson, a SPORTS ILLUSTRATED cover boy in college at Navy, was nicknamed the "Admiral." Now one of the NBA's most respected veterans (seen here playing against Karl Malone), it would be his job to take Tim under his wing.

Tim was thrilled to be the NBA's number-one pick in 1997. David Robinson was thrilled to find his new teammate was so committed to winning.

What a great situation. David Robinson would return at 100 percent in 1997–98, which meant that Tim would not only have a superstar teammate, but one who could show him how to be a dominant big man in the NBA. Tim would not be expected to "save" the franchise; he could develop at his own pace.

Right after the draft, Tim got a call from Robinson, inviting him to his home in Aspen, Colorado. They spent several days together, hanging out, talking basketball, playing one-on-one, lifting weights, and becoming friends. "I worked him pretty hard and he never complained," Robinson says.

Robinson marveled at Tim's great hands, his aggressiveness, and his quickness. Like most people, Robinson initially thought that Tim's easy, measured personality meant that he might lack quickness on the court. The "Admiral"—as the Naval Academy graduate is called—learned the hard way that there is nothing slow about how Tim's body moves. In their one-on-one competitions, the rookie sank his ship time and time again.

High Praise From
Big Dave

"He shows a lot of composure that is really beyond his age, and has an understanding of the game I can really appreciate."

"Tim really looks comfortable out there. He's putting up numbers to rival any power forward in the league."

"It makes my job so much easier when he can score like that on the block late in the game...the better he is, the more my game is going to flow."

Twin Towers

chapter 12

> *"We're smart enough players to figure out how much to complement each other without clashing too much."*
>
> — **TIM DUNCAN**

The "Twin Towers" concept had been tried before in the NBA without success, and Spurs coach Gregg Popovich knew it. If history was any kind of teacher, playing two natural centers together was a recipe for disaster. Wilt Chamberlain and Nate Thurmond, Bill Cartwright and Marvin Webster, Ralph Sampson and Hakeem Olajuwon—all superb individual players—played side-by-side in the past and just ended up getting in each other's way. Popovich was convinced that *his* Twin Towers were different. Never before had two centers on the same team possessed the skills to pop out and be effective away from the basket. David Robinson and Tim Duncan definitely were.

Of course, much depended on the other Spurs. Avery Johnson, the team's veteran point guard, ranked among the top ball distributors in the game. Vinny Del Negro, a good all-around performer, started in the backcourt beside him. The shooting forwards, Scan Elliott and Chuck Person, were both coming off serious injuries, but had performed brilliantly in past seasons. Will Perdue, a veteran enforcer, was an excellent backup center. Jaren Jackson, Cory Alexander, Carl Herrara, and Monty Williams—all valuable contributors— were also in the rotation. It was a good group, but there were definitely some question marks.

As for the fans, they were rooting for Tim to help the Spurs break a

Tim's play in the pivot enabled David Robinson (50) to bring his game outside.

record. In 1989–90, Robinson had a fabulous rookie year and helped the team improve by an unprecedented 35 wins. If the Spurs could win 56 games, they would break their own NBA mark.

players don't make mid-range shots anymore," says coach Gregg Popovich, who devised this strategy. "They can shoot threes, and they can go to the hole and be athletic, but hardly anyone wants to stop in the middle these days. So that's exactly what we try to make them do."

Over the final 36 games, the Spurs fashioned a sparkling 31–5 record and finished with the best record in the Western Conference. Meanwhile, Tim seemed to be getting better by the week. He was playing defense all over the court, and finding a dozen different ways to score. Suddenly, it dawned on everyone: with Michael Jordan retired, Tim was probably the best player in basketball!

Tim finished the year sixth in scoring, fifth in rebounding, seventh in blocked shots, and ninth in minutes played. He was voted to both the All-NBA and All-Defensive first teams, and finished third behind Karl Malone and Alonzo Mourning in the MVP voting.

Tim's greatest contribution to the Spurs, however, was not evident until playoff time. That is when he saw the fruits of his labor. That is when he finally was sure that his teammates were thinking like he was. They were focused, relaxed, and supremely confident. When something went wrong, they dealt with it. If an important call went against them, they regrouped quickly. And when the game was on the line and the team needed a bucket, each player felt he could hit the big shot. The Spurs had been called the "best team in basketball" before, but this time they truly believed it.

That is why the 1999 playoffs seemed like little more than a coronation ceremony. The Spurs rolled over the Timberwolves, Lakers, and Trailblazers to reach the NBA Finals with a total of just one defeat. There they faced the New York Knicks, a team decimated by injuries but dangerous nonetheless. New York's two best players, Allan Houston and Lattrell Sprewell, were among the few shooters in the league who could score from medium range, which was considered San Antonio's "Achilles heel."

In the first two games of the series, Tim took over. He scored at will, and on defense he stepped out to harass New York's jump-shooters into hurrying their shots. After dropping the first two games, the Knicks managed to win Game Three, but they still were powerless to stop Tim. The Spurs won the next two games to close out the series. Tim, who averaged 27.5 points and 14 rebounds against the Knicks, was named

The twin towers display some impressive hardware . David Robinson holds up the NBA championship trophy and Tim shows off his NBA Finals MVP award. The Spurs beat the Knicks in 5 games to win the title.

NBA Finals MVP. After 26 years, San Antonio had its first pro basketball championship.

While the rest of the Spurs danced around the court at Madison Square Garden and exchanged hugs and high fives, Tim grabbed a video camera and started taping the celebration. When the team returned to Texas, 250,000 people showed up for one of history's most unique victory parades. The Spurs floated through the city on special boats, waving to fans who lined San Antonio's famous Riverwalk. Tim was filming this, too.

He has quite a sense of history for such a young man. But he has an eye on the future, too. Tim knows that everyone will be gunning for the Spurs now, and that he will have to continue to improve his game, especially as Robinson's declines.

Tim is sure he can do it. More importantly, he is certain that his fellow Spurs can keep improving, too. "We'll be ready," Tim says with his typical cool confidence. "We'll be right back up there."

Index